T0193437

Order this book online at www.trafford.com
or email orders@trafford.com

Most Trafford titles are also available at major online book retailers.

Trafford
PUBLISHING®   www.trafford.com
North America & international
toll-free: 1 888 232 4444 (USA & Canada)
fax: 812 355 4082

Our mission is to efficiently provide the world's finest, most comprehensive book publishing service, enabling every author to experience success. To find out how to publish your book, your way, and have it available worldwide, visit us online at www.trafford.com

Because of the dynamic nature of the Internet, any web addresses or links contained in this book may have changed since publication and may no longer be valid. The views expressed in this work are solely those of the author and do not necessarily reflect the views of the publisher, and the publisher hereby disclaims any responsibility for them.

Any people depicted in stock imagery provided by Getty Images are models, and such images are being used for illustrative purposes only.
Certain stock imagery © Getty Images.

ISBN: 978-1-4907-9785-4 (sc)

ISBN: 978-1-4907-9784-7 (e)

Print information available on the last page.

Trafford rev. 08/11/2020

JACKIE'S NEW TOY

Felipe Cofreros Ph.D.

Jackie, Brownie, and Tipsie were good friends. They lived in the same neighborhood and studied in the same school. They usually walked to school every morning.

One morning, Jackie showed his new toy to Tipsie and Brownie. "Guys, Grandma gave me a new toy. Look!" Jackie said. "Wow! It's beautiful." Said Tipsie.

Brownie looked at it. "Let me see it." He reached for it and said, "Let me bury it, then the two of you will look for it."

"Wait... we still have time to play with it. How about if we take turns in burying and digging for it?" Jackie said. "Let's see who among us could find it in the shortest time."
"Okay." Tipsie and Brownie answered in chorus. Tipsie gave back the toy to Jackie.

Jackie went behind a fence
and hid the bone under a bush.
Then, he called his friends
to sniff and dig for it.

They took turns in burying and digging the bone. They enjoyed the game so much that they forgot about the time.

"Gosh! It's almost time for our class," exclaimed Tipsie. "Here, keep your toy, Jackie and let's run to school."

"Sorry I asked to play with my new toy, guys. I shouldn't have shown it to you." Jackie apologized. "No need to say sorry, we don't blame you," Brownie said. "We are all in this." The three friends ran to school.

Exercise 1: YES or NO

_____ 1. Jackie's new toy was a bone.

_____ 2. The three friends skipped class to play.

_____ 3. The toy was from Jackie's grandmother.

_____ 4. Tipsie told his friends to run to school.

_____ 5. Brownie was angry at Jackie.

Exercise 2: Encircle the best answer.

1. **Tipsie, Brownie, and Jackie were _____.**
   a. friends   b. brothers   c. classmates

2. **Jackie has a new _____.**
   a. bag   b. friend c. toy

3. **The three friends usually _____ to school.**
   a. walked   b. took a bus   c. jumped

4. **Jackie buried the bone under the _____.**
   a. house   b. bush   c. fence

5. **The three friends were _____.**
   a. tired b. happy c. sad

Exercise 3: Arrange the events by numbering 1 to 5.

_____ The three friends ran to school.

_____ Jackie buried the toy under the fence.

_____ Jackie showed his new toy to his friends.

_____ They took turns in looking for the bone.

_____ The three friends were walking to school.

Exercise 4: Describe the picture

1. _____

2. _____

Exercise 4: Color Jackie and his friends.

"JACKIE'S NEW TOY" is an eye-catching book that contains a story and more. This book is geared for pre-school children ages three and up. With the simple story and powerful comprehension questions, "JACKIE'S NEW TOY" engages the child by focusing concentration, improving comprehension, stimulating thought and galvanizing imagination.

This book is intended for use in the pre-school classroom. The students can answer questions, generate their own questions, act out the story or continue the story. It can be read to two and three year old students, while the older students can relate to the higher level activities.

Although the book is designed for classroom use, it can be used in the home, and setup in the book gives children a chance to relate to their parents while discussing the story.

Printed in the United States
By Bookmasters